The Parts Inside of Me

Written by
Shelly Johnson, MA LMHC

Illustrated by
Mark Savona

Foreword by
Michi Rose, PhD, MAT, LMSW

"*The Parts Inside of Me* is a delightful book that demonstrates the beauty of being open and curious to our inner world and how we all have unique and wonderful parts of our own."

- SETH KOPALD, PhD, M.Ed, Certified IFS Practitioner, Ann Arbor, Michigan

"This book is a loving tribute to the complexity and depth of our internal worlds. It shows beautiful examples of specific parts which may be similar to those of many readers, but are completely individual and unique, as all our parts are. An inspirational and insightful poetic story, *The Parts Inside of Me* is a wonderful clinical tool to use with young people, adults, families and groups to fully illustrate the internal family system which resides within us all, and to stimulate discussion, exploration and curiosity regarding one's own family inside."

- TANIS ALLEN, LMSW, ACSW, Certified IFS Therapist, Ann Arbor, Michigan

"Shelly Johnson's imagery and poetry tell the story of her inner world. This poignant portrayal encourages us all to look inside and explore our own family of parts with sensitivity and compassion. This book is a wonderful addition to the Internal Family Systems growing library and humanity in general."

- LISA SPIEGEL, MA, LMHC, Author of *Internal Family Systems Therapy with Children*

"Shelly Johnson's *The Parts Inside of Me* is a beautifully written primer about our internal world of sub-personalities. Designed to be understood by children and adults, it opens up that world in each of us for discovery, unconditional love and healing."

- BILL KAVANAGH, LCSW CADC (Retired), San Miguel de Allende, Mexico

"A very personal account of discovery and awareness of the many Parts we all have in our internal worlds—and how the welcoming of those Parts by the Self can create calm. A comforting introduction to the IFS model for people of all ages."

- JAN CAMPANELLI, PhD, LPC, IFS Therapist, Milwaukee, Wisconsin

"A beautiful invitation to identify, honor and embrace all of our parts and aspects. Inclusivity within society, cannot happen until we become internally inclusive. This book invites us in the right direction."

- JEFF BROWN, Author of *Grounded Spirituality*

"A brave, unique, and timely book that invites us all to journey inward with curiosity and love--to dare to visit the unknown, unconscious places within us, and in so doing, transform them into a world of playful discovery and increased inner harmony."

- ANNA HUCKABEE TULL, Author of *Living the Deeper YES*

"Shelly Johnson has organized a quick tour of her — of everyone's — mind. It is scary in there; at the same time that it is uplifting! But, more than anything, it is human, caring, and optimistic. Take the tour with her and explore your own innermost feelings — realizing that you can return as often as you wish, always seeking more and flying higher...while having fun! Just like life."

- DR. STANTON PEELE, PhD, JD, Author of *Outgrowing Addiction,* and contributing writer for *Psychology Today* and *The Huffington Post*

"Exquisitely written, *The Parts Inside of Me* invites whimsical connection with the most sacred members of our inner world. A delight for readers of all ages! As Shelly's tale artistically unfolds, captivating images guide us to discover the cherished gifts of the internal universe."

- GINA ABBEDUTO, MS, LCPC, Certified IFS Therapist, Henderson, Nevada

The Parts
Inside of Me

Written by
Shelly Johnson, MA LMHC

Illustrated by
Mark Savona

Foreword by Michi Rose, PhD, MAT, LMSW

Archway Publishing books may be ordered through booksellers or by contacting:

Archway Publishing
1663 Liberty Drive
Bloomington, IN 47403
www.archwaypublishing.com
1 (888) 242-5904

Interior Image Credit: Mark Savona

ISBN: 978-1-4808-8625-4 (sc)
ISBN: 978-1-4808-8626-1 (hc)
ISBN: 978-1-4808-8627-8 (e)

Print information available on the last page.

Archway Publishing rev. date: 1/20/2020

DEDICATION

For the gifted Self that is resident within ALL of US. And, most especially, I dedicate this book to the soulful and spirited goodness of each and every member of the IFS Community...

TOGETHER,
WE can love our Parts and our world back into balance.

"If you love what's in your way, they will transform"
~ Dr. Richard Schwartz

FOREWORD

"I believe that there is a divine spark in every human being, although it may be buried deeply."

~ Michi Rose, PhD, MAT, LMSW

"*The Parts Inside of Me*" is a delightful journey inside the mind of the author.

Shelly Johnson is a practitioner of "Internal Family Systems," a path of self-discovery that increases awareness of the different "parts" of one's personality or psyche. Shelly has also served as a PA for level 1 trainees of the model.

This book is an intimate, at times comical, description of parts that make up the inner landscape of her mind, body, and spirit. It offers a picturesque description of her inward journey.

Every part has its own personality, story, perspective, role, and feelings. Each part contributes to our daily living, thought patterns, emotional experiences, and functioning.

This book encourages readers to accompany these characters on their journey; it is also intended to inspire people to be curious about their own parts.

Through uncovering the different parts of themselves, people make the unconscious conscious. This is a creative path to knowing oneself and others.

Shelly's intention is to help people identify, access, and understand the parts of themselves to bring about better inner balance and harmony.

May this book's insightful wisdom invite you into this creative way of looking at the psyche to discover deeper self-understanding.

~ Michi Rose

ACKNOWLEDGMENTS

There are so many to thank that had an extended hand in this.....

GOD

To *Dick Schwartz* for creating such a distinct, respectful, and elegant therapeutic model that has the healing capacity of changing the world...it already is, one Part at a time. Your heart, your vision, your passion and compassion, does not go unnoticed. You are a pioneer in the Zeitgeist occurring within the field of psychotherapy and you truly practice what you preach. You have modeled for each of us, that IFS isn't just a therapy model or an approach for self-growth work, but it is a way of life that helps a person reclaim the totality of who they are. Thank you for your tireless devotion in listening so intently .....to your own Parts and to the many Parts of others that helped inform the evolution of IFS. And lastly, thank you so much for believing in the message and essence of this book and encouraging its release!

To *Michi Rose*, (often known in the IFS community as the Godmother of IFS) for continuing to inspire so many therapists, practitioners, and students in your teachings. You collaborated so closely with Dick Schwartz in the early developmental stages of the model and are credited for bringing a lot of the spiritual components to its creation. Thank you for the enormous amount of time (literally DECADES) you have spent teaching this model and for helping shape it into the extraordinary gift it has become for so many of us today. Your humility, grace, self-energy, and compassion is in a league of its own!

To my incredibly 'talented' Illustrator, *Mark Savona*, who has brought a creative brilliance to this book; I could not be more grateful. Out of 40+ applicants from Illustrators (nationally and internationally) interested in the project, this Scholastic Illustrator's portfolio submission catapulted him to the top of our list! Mark, your psychological depth, range of artistic skills, and astute attention to detail is a rare find. You saw this as a strong movement and cause to stand behind in illuminating the transformational power and expansive healing impact of IFS. ALL the late hours you spent in conference with our Creative Consultant and myself this past year, to really capture how you wanted to illustrate the concepts, was a phenomenal and rewarding process to be connected with. You have been my wing man in this project. Your hard work, professionalism and commitment to excellence is so very much appreciated!

To my remarkable Creative Consultant, *Tiffany Sinnott*, who always kept a steady hand as a liaison between Mark and I. You had a very clear idea of what you were looking to see and yet were so open to the Illustrator's interpretation of the work. Your unique animation background and illustrative experience made you a perfect fit to assist as my Creative Consultant. You were very dedicated to standing behind this project and pushing the mission of spreading IFS to a greater mass of people. Your contributions are significant in creating the initial rough sketch designs/ideas for the interior storyboard, which served as a blueprint for referencing. You have been my wing woman in this project, and I have enjoyed every minute of it!

To my 'beyond gifted' Trainers: *Cece Sykes, Gretchen King, Pamela Krause, Cathy Curtis, Toni Herbine-Blank* (These individuals have influenced my learning of the model in a major way). I have so much gratitude for your service and leadership in spreading IFS to so many eager students of the model; I have been in 'awe' of your tenacious work, mentorship, and how much you embody the spirit of IFS. I've witnessed how much you pour your heart out into these trainings and I am so honored to be in your loving, energetic orbit!

To ALL Lead and Assistant Trainers: I think very highly of the Lead and Assistant Trainers (those I've been trained by and those I have yet to meet). Each of you are purposely positioned on the frontlines of educating students and building a wider global presence for IFS; it is hard work that you've committed your career and your lives to. Constantly teaching and interacting with learning participants requires an immense amount of self-energy and a very open heart; this alone speaks 'volumes' in terms of the caliber of professionals that you are!

To *Christina Johnson*: You are an amazing Psychotherapist and have been a great sounding board for this book project. I want to especially thank you for your rough sketch ideas for the cover art with use of various doors to represent Parts...Very Clever!

Other special thanks to: *Dr. Maureen Dion, Derek Scott, Dr. Janet Shepherd, Joanna Lawson, Julie Honeycutt, Alex Solaro, Lisa Bourdon, Gina Abbeduto, Seth Kopald, Tanis Allen, Lisa Spiegel, Bill Kavanagh, Jan Campanelli, Jeff Brown, Anna Huckabee Tull, Madeleine Warren, and Dr. Stanton Peele.* Each of you are 'phenomenal' professionals who have made a special impact on my Parts and have helped me learn to love them as equals rather than disown them.

To ALL of my Family, Friends, Fellow PAs, and IFS Colleagues who have supported my professional work and personal journey of self growth. I love you ALL!

Deep inside my body
and all around my head,
lives a circle of beings
who sometimes feel misread.

I'm here to give some time
to sit with them awhile,
and listen deeper within,
to meet the ones exiled.

But before I come close
to those I keep at bay,
I'll greet mighty Protectors
who guard along the way.

There's a legion of Parts
who need some room to grow,
and tell so many stories
of which I'd love to know.

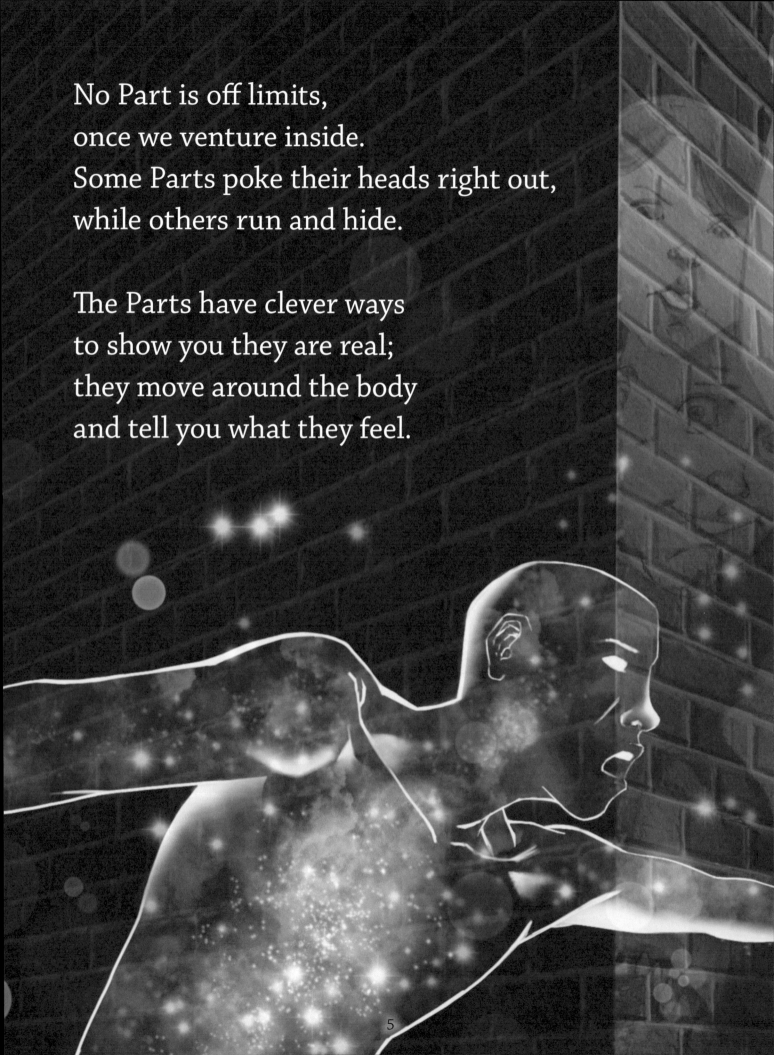

No Part is off limits,
once we venture inside.
Some Parts poke their heads right out,
while others run and hide.

The Parts have clever ways
to show you they are real;
they move around the body
and tell you what they feel.

Our Parts are here to stay
and won't always agree.
It's impossible to choose
our inner family.

I have a Part in me
who cannot stand the rest;
it often tries to flood me,
believing it knows best.

Come see the one who's sad,
that weeps and cries at night,
or the one under covers
that lives its days in fright.

One wants for me to go
and one asks me to stay.
One bulldozes through others
to get out of its way.

I have a Part in me
that's quick to raise its brow,
and asks me repeatedly,
"Whose side are you on now!"

There's one who wants to fight
and tightens up its fists;
its rage is an inferno
that no-one can resist.

NO-
ONE'S
LISTENING!

One worries all the time
and cannot sit too still;
it rumbles in my stomach.
Believe me, it's no thrill!

One carries a long list
and has a bossy voice;
it tells me I do things wrong,
as if I have no choice.

I have a sneaky Part
who looks for an escape;
it dances with disaster,
yet caught in its own wake.

I have a Part that says,
"I simply will not budge;"
it does whatever it wants
and sometimes holds a grudge.

Beneath all the layers,
there's a Part that holds shame,
while another Part points out
accomplices to blame.

There's a Part speaking up,
scolding me for a mess;
it pushes all my buttons,
and does not let me rest!

I have a Part that still
obsesses over things;
it really hasn't a clue
how much chaos it brings.

Protectors soften back
in efforts to disarm,
after Exiles promise Self
not to pull the alarm.

A Part feels embarrassed
that now you see its flaws,
and it let you in this close
without taking a pause.

See my adventure Part,
chasing the next new thrill;
it lives its life on the edge
until it rolls downhill.

There is a Part of me
who wants to change its route;
it second guesses my worth
and tries to snuff me out.

Where is the know-it-all?
That Part lives in here too;
it fears others finding out
just how little it knew.

Part of me wears a cape
and is swift on its feet;
its nature is to rescue
and nurture your relief.

I have a Part in me
that can follow the pack,
or will spread itself too thin
like a human doormat.

There's a Part that misses
the way it used to be;
it wishes you were still here,
although time set you free.

How about my shy Part
that carries so much doubt
or the tingly Part that numbs,
and tries to take me out!

I have a Part in me
that chases affection;
it's desperate to belong
to ward off rejection.

I have a quiet Part
that hurts on the inside;
it keeps too many secrets,
in order to survive.

Hear the Part that giggles
and laughs without a care.
Some Parts hide behind a smile
when they're afraid to share.

Bless the Part that struggles
to understand its faith;
it seeks for a higher truth
beyond reason or fate.

A game of hide and seek
is sometimes how it feels,
but nothing comes to surface
until you reach the peels.

And if a Part gets stuck,
it often has a fear.
Bringing curiosity,
allows for us to hear.

We have a wiser Self
that stays above the fray;
it's able to take the lead
on any given day.

I now know its presence;
its energy is calm,
and it aims to help my Parts
find ways to get along.

There are times that I feel
lost inside my own head,
but it's worth the giant leap
to love myself instead.

I can witness for YOU
like YOU witness for ME,
and WE can bring compassion
towards inner harmony.

I am the way I am.
It's clear for all to see,
how much I completely love
the Parts inside of me.

The world could be a kind place;
what a gift if we can believe--
that the Parts you see in others,
might reside in you and me.

About the Author

Shelly Johnson is an IFS Therapist who has trained extensively with top clinical leaders, to practice the Internal Family Systems Model of Psychotherapy. She has also served as a PA on the training staff for level one IFS participants. Shelly, who is a champion of children's education, literacy, and mental health awareness, resides in Des Moines, Iowa with her family and loyal furry companion.